HOW TO USE T~~HIS~~ BOOK

When you have a rules question, tur~~n~~
of the course to which your questi~~
and its answer will be readily found~~

If your question relates to the te~~
fairway or rough - page 4; and so on. ~~Page~~
contains answers common to all parts of the course.

WHERE IS YOUR BALL?

OTHER SUBJECTS:

THE TEE

I'll go first Doug because I'm on a lower handicap than you.

No you won't Russell. The order of play is determined by the starter. As I was called first I am the first to play. Until you win a hole I have the honour.

Should start of play be not under starters control, the order of play would be determined by casting lots (flip a coin).

Ball in play - a ball is only in play on any hole, when a completed stroke at the players ball, has been made.

Ball falls from tee (moving ball)
Swing aborted	- no penalty – re-tee
Swing completed	- no penalty but count 1 stroke for completed swing – ball is in play and cannot be re-teed without penalty

Hitting from wrong teeing area (Swing is not counted - stroke must be replayed)
In front of markers	- penalty 2 strokes
Outside of markers (stance may be outside - not ball)	- penalty 2 strokes
More than two club lengths behind markers	- penalty 2 strokes

Failure to replay from correct area - disqualification

Practice swing - ball (not yet in play) knocked from tee - no penalty - re-tee free

Is it alright to practice putting while waiting for the group in front to clear the tee?

Yes Russell. Chipping and putting is allowed (unless a local rule prohibits) on or to the green completed, or the next tee area, or a practice area, so long as we don't hold up play. It is also allowed on or near the first tee area before starting a round. Practice is not allowed from a hazard.

FURTHER ANSWERS ON PAGE 30

THROUGH THE GREEN

PROBLEM	FAIRWAY (closely mown area only)	ROUGH (not so closely mown)
Animal Holes/Scratchings made by - burrowing animals, reptiles & birds - non-burrowing animals	Ball in, or swing or normal stance interfered by - free drop - 1 club length *	
	No relief	
Ball Moved	See page 30	
Bare Patches	No relief	
Casual Water - ball found	For relief to be available water must be visible *before or after* taking normal stance. Mushy ground provides no relief nor does dew or frost. Free drop - 1 club length *	
- ball lost in water	Free drop - 1 club length (relief is from estimated last entry point) *	
Cleaning Ball - when taking relief - not in relief situations	Permitted - no penalty Penalty 1 stroke	
Dirt/Soil/Sand	Removing to improve lie, stance, swing etc - Penalty 2 strokes	
Dropping Ball (page 42) *	1 club length drops are measured from the nearest point of relief to where the ball lies, or if lost, from the estimated point where the ball last entered the abnormal ground or obstruction (which is not nearer the hole and is not in a hazard or on a green). **Note:** Relief from abnormal ground, including, animal holes, casual water, G.U.R. and also from immovable obstructions is not permitted if a stroke is not possible because of some other factor, such as a tree or roots or if the interference results only from taking an abnormal stance, swing or direction of play. (See page 44)	
* Nearest Point of Relief (Page 24)		
Grass Clippings - piled for removal - not for removal	Free drop - 1 club length * Loose impediment relief (page 36)	
Ground Under Repair (page 10)	Free drop 1 club length *	
Identifying Ball - marking, lifting, and replacing (must give marker/fellow competitor opportunity to observe)	- permitted - but 1 stroke penalty if done without giving opportunity to observe or if done when not necessary	
Immovable Obstructions (page 40)	Free drop - 1 club length *	

Improving: Lie, Stance, Area of Intended Swing, Dropping Area, Line of Play	In "fairly" taking stance - no penalty Moving loose impediments and movable obstructions - no penalty Other improvements - during a completed stroke - no penalty Other - penalty 2 strokes
Loose Impediments (P.36) (natural objects)	Remove - no penalty If ball moves as a result of removing - penalty 1 stroke and replace ball
Movable Obstructions (P.38) (artificial objects)	Remove - no penalty If ball moves - no penalty - replace ball
Paths & Roads - soil/clay/dirt - artificial (P.40)	No relief Free drop - 1 club length *
Playing Moving Ball	Penalty - 2 strokes excepting that if ball commenced to move after back swing commenced there is no penalty. If you caused the ball to move see page 30 for possible "ball moved" penalty.
Plugged Ball	A free drop at nearest point of relief is allowed for a ball plugged in its own plug hole, but only if the ball is on a closely mown part of the course. Grass paths between holes will give relief if mown to fairway level.
Sprinkler Heads (P.40)	Free drop - 1 club length *
Staked Trees	Free drop from stake and also from tree if local rule - 1 club length *
Unplayable Ball	See page 44
Water Hazard Overflow	Is casual water from which free relief is available
Wheel Tracks	No relief from pull carts, motor carts, or machinery tracks (most clubs grant relief from machinery tracks under local rules)
Wrong Ball Played - a ball substituted.... - not your ball....	(Whether intentionally or not) - Count stroke - play as lies - penalty 2 strokes Don't count stroke - re-play- penalty 2 strokes - failure to re-play - disqualification

FURTHER ANSWERS ON PAGE 30

FAIRWAY & ROUGH

4

SAND & WATER

As there is casual water on the green between my ball and the hole, and sand in front of my ball, I must be entitled to relief.

Sorry Russell, while your ball is off the green you are not entitled to relief from casual water on the green. As for the sand in front of your ball, you know you cannot remove that without penalty. Sand is only a loose impediment when it is on the green . You can repair plug marks on the green whether your ball is on or not.

GRASS CLIPPINGS

My ball is in grass clippings so I'm entitled to a free drop.

No Russell - those clippings are not there for subsequent removal but are clearly there to mulch the tree. As cut grass is a loose impediment you may remove the clippings but be careful that your ball does not move.

SECOND BALL

Surely I can drop from this path Doug?

No you can't Russell. It's made of only soil & clay - no artificial materials.

If you disagree you may play the ball as it lies and also a dropped ball and have the matter decided by the committee

INSTANT ANSWERS - FAIRWAY & ROUGH - PAGES 4 & 30

My ball's covered in mud - I'll wipe it on the green.

Thul's OK Russell, so long as you're not deliberately testing the surface of the green.

Now that I have marked my ball may I clean it?

No Russell you cannot. You marked your ball because it was in the way of my swing, not because you were entitled to relief. As you are not on the green you are not permitted to clean the ball. And don't put it in your pocket as that could constitute cleaning the ball.

My ball was plugged and is now covered in mud. May I clean it?

Yes Russell. As you have lifted it in a relief drop situation you are entitled to clean the ball.

My ball looks lost in this G.U.R. area Doug. What should I do?

Fortunately Russell you are entitled to a free drop with another ball. Had we not seen the ball go in there you would have to go back and play a ball under the lost ball rules. You must drop within 1 club length of the nearest point of relief from where you estimate the ball last entered the G.U.R.

Look Doug, here's my drive. I'll pick up the ball I hit when I thought this was lost in the G.U.R.

You can't do that. When you played the second ball, it became your ball in play. Clearly you were not 'virtually certain' the first one was lost in the G.U.R., so you should have gone back to the tee and replayed. Now you have a 2 stroke penalty, and having played from a wrong place with a 150m advantage, you will be disqualified if you don't go back and replay your drive.

Surely I can drop from these wheel tracks Doug?

Sorry Russell. Only local rules can provide wheel track relief. This club allows relief from machinery tracks, but as this is a motorised cart track you must play the ball as it lies.

ABNORMAL GROUND (G.U.R.)

Areas so designated with white posts or paint lines, and areas containing casual water, ground under repair, holes, casts, runways made by burrowing animals, reptiles or birds, and green keepers grass cuttings or tree trimmings piled for removal.

A ball is in G.U.R. when any part is inside or touches the Ground Under Repair. Anything growing in G.U.R. is part of G.U.R. even if extending beyond the boundary.

Ball in, or swing or normal stance interfered by.

Relief - Free drop 1 club length from nearest point of relief (which is not nearer the hole, and is not in a hazard or on a green) excepting, that:
- (i) Where making a stroke is not possible because of some other factor such as a tree or roots (outside of the G.U.R. area), or
- (ii) The obstruction only interferes as a result of taking an abnormal stance, swing or direction of play, then . . . free relief is not available (see page 44).

Ball lost in G.U.R.	- free drop - relief is from estimated final entry point. If not "Virtually certain" that the ball entered and remained in the abnormal ground, free relief is not available.
Ball in G.U.R.	- play as is or free drop.
Bush or tree in G.U.R.	- ball in bush is in G.U.R. even though not on ground.
Compulsory G.U.R.	- failure to drop outside of designated compulsory G.U.R. - penalty - 2 strokes
Course Renovations	- Aeration holes on greens are not work in progress and no relief is available.
Grass clippings	- free drop if piled for removal, loose impediment relief if not (page 36).
G.U.R. not designated	- where ground staff have commenced course maintenance but not marked work area as G.U.R. such as holes dug, timber cut for removal, such areas can be treated as G.U.R.
Stakes delineating G.U.R.	- can be either movable or immovable obstructions depending on how solidly embedded. Easily moved stakes are often declared immovable obstructions under local rules.
Wheel tracks	- neither pull cart, motorised cart or machinery tracks are G.U.R. and no relief is available. Local rules often allow for relief from machinery tracks.

FURTHER ANSWERS ON PAGE 30

A
B
N
O
R
M
A
L

G
R
O
U
N
D

BUNKER

The margin of a bunker extends downwards – not upwards.

A ball is in a bunker when any part touches the bunker.

Topic	Detail	Ruling
Animal Holes/Scratchings – made by – burrowing animals, reptiles & birds – non-burrowing animals	– ball in or swing or normal stance interfered by	– free drop (in bunker) – 1 club length * – No relief
Ball Moves	– when removing movable obstruction – in searching for ball in sand	– no penalty – no penalty
Casual Water – ball lost in or ball retrievable		– replace ball – replace ball
		– free drop (in bunker) 1 club length * If full relief not available, drop in place of least water, or for 1 stroke penalty drop (1) behind bunker, keeping spot where ball lay in a straight line between drop point and the hole, or (2) from where previous shot was played.
Dropping Ball (page 42) * 1 club length drops are measured from the **nearest point of relief** (within the bunker) to where the ball lies, not nearer the hole. If the ball is lost in casual water within the bunker, then **(n.p.o.r.)** from the estimated point where the ball last entered the water.		
Grassy Islands in Bunker – are not part of bunker		– Ball can be played where lies, or relief taken under unplayable ball options (page 44)
Grounding Club or touching ground or loose impediments with the hand or club – searching for ball – other (when ball is in hazard)		– no penalty – penalty 2 strokes excepting, that where the lie of the ball is not improved, nor the hazard condition deemed to have been tested, grounding a club or touching with the hand in the following situations incurs no penalty: – to prevent falling, removing movable obstructions, measuring, picking up or placing ball (where permitted) smoothing sand or soil after failing to exit (provided swing area, stance or line of play are not improved)
Identifying Ball – marking, lifting, and replacing (must give marker/fellow competitor opportunity to observe)		– permitted – but 1 stroke penalty if done without giving opportunity to observe or if done when not necessary
Immovable Obstructions (page 40)		– free drop – (in bunker) 1 club length * or for 1 stroke penalty outside the bunker keeping drop point and where ball lay in line with the flag.

TO RULES QUESTIONS - BUNKER

Loose Impediments (natural objects) page 36 - to move or remove - in searching for ball	- no penalty and replace impediment (small part of ball may be left exposed)
- in back swing - in down swing (the golf stroke) - other accidental	- penalty 2 strokes - no penalty - no penalty unless lie or area of intended swing or stance improved.
- other	- penalty 2 strokes
Movable Obstructions (artificial objects) page 38	- remove - no penalty
Playing Moving Ball	- penalty - 2 strokes excepting that if ball commenced to move after back swing started there is no penalty. If you caused the ball to move see page 30 for possible "ball moved" penalty.
Plugged Ball - in bunker - in grass outside	- no relief - free relief only if on the closely mown area
Rake outside bunker stopping ball from rolling into bunker	- remove rake and if ball rolls, place in original position, or in nearest spot outside the bunker where ball will rest - no penalty
Raking prior to playing stroke - not done to obtain advantage	- no penalty
Searching for Ball - probing, touching, raking	- no penalty - ball must be restored to original position (small part of ball may be left exposed).
Stones	- removable only if authorised by local rule
Unplayable Ball	- refer to page 44
Wrong Ball Played - a ball substituted.... - not your ball....	(Whether intentionally or not) - Count stroke - play as lies - penalty 2 strokes Don't count stroke - re-play- penalty 2 strokes - failure to re-play - disqualification

FURTHER ANSWERS ON PAGE 30

BUNKER

11

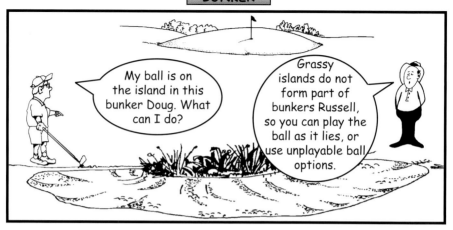

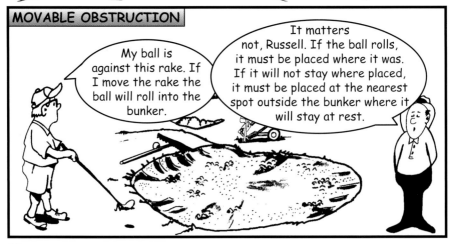

IMMOVABLE OBSTRUCTION

My ball is against a drainage outlet in this bunker. Do I get a drop?

Yes Russell. Immovable Obstructions in bunkers provide relief. If your ball was in a water hazard you would get no relief.

WRONG BALL

That's not my ball I've just hit from the bunker. I suppose that's another penalty.

Yes Russell - 2 strokes. You should have identified your ball. The rules now permit the same marking and lifting procedures as elsewhere on the course.

MARKING BALL

If I mark my ball in this bunker so that you can play, I will be left with a hole to play from.

Don't worry Russell. After I have played, I will restore your lie to what it now is.

Water hazards are defined by either yellow or red posts or lines.

WATER HAZARD

Stakes defining hazards are obstructions within the hazard.

A ball is in a water hazard when any part is inside the margin of the hazard.
Options - Play as lies (if ball located) or for 1 stroke penalty take relief.

The relief options from red posted areas (called lateral hazards) include two more options than from yellow posted hazards. **The principal options for relief from water hazards are:**

(1) Drop ball behind hazard (no limit on distance) keeping point where ball last entered the hazard between the drop point and the flag.

(2) Play from where previous shot was played.

For red posted hazards the additional options are; drop within two club lengths of:

(3) The point where the ball last entered the hazard not nearer the hole.

(4) A point on the opposite side of the hazard - opposite to the point where the hazard was last crossed equidistant from the hole (see page 25).

INSTANT ANSWERS

Abnormal Ground, Ground Under Repair	- no relief
Assumption that ball is in hazard	- it must be known or virtually certain that the ball entered the hazard, else must be played as a lost ball
Ball Fails to exit hazard or enters another water hazard	- play as lies or for penalty (1 stroke) play from where the previous stroke was played or choose from the options available when the ball first entered the hazard.
Ball Lost in Water Hazard	- same options as ball in water hazard
Ball Moves - when removing movable obstructions - in searching in loose impediments - in replacing loose impediments	- no penalty - replace ball - penalty 1 stroke - replace ball - no penalty - replace ball
Bridge Over Hazard	- is in hazard but can ground club on bridge
Casual Water	- no relief from any water in a water hazard

Grounding Club or touching ground, water, or loose impediments with the hand or club	
- searching for ball	- no penalty
- other (when ball is in hazard)	- penalty 2 strokes
excepting, that where the lie of the ball is not improved, nor the hazard condition deemed to have been tested, grounding a club or touching with the hand in the following situations incurs no penalty: to prevent falling, removing movable obstructions, measuring, picking up or placing ball (where permitted, smoothing sand or soil after failing to exit (provided swing area, stance or line of play are not improved)	
Identifying Ball – marking, lifting, and replacing (must give marker/fellow competitor opportunity to observe)	- permitted – but 1 stroke penalty if done without giving opportunity to observe or if done when not necessary
Immovable Obstructions (page 40)	- no relief
Loose Impediments (page 36)	
- to move or remove in searching for ball	- no penalty but must replace impediment (small part of ball may be left exposed)
- in back swing	- penalty 2 strokes
- in down swing (the golf stroke)	- no penalty
- other accidental	- no penalty unless lie or area of intended swing or stance improved
- other	- penalty 2 strokes
Movable Obstructions (artificial objects) page 38	- remove – no penalty
Playing Moving Ball	- no penalty to hit while moving in water unless stroke was delayed for current or wind to improve position.
Plugged Ball	- no relief
Stake Missing – Ball Clearly in Hazard	- ball is considered to be in hazard
Stakes Delineating Hazard – easily removable	- remove unless declared immovable by local rule
– not easily removable	- no relief if ball is in hazard
Unplayable Ball – ball in water hazard cannot be declared an "unplayable ball", only water hazard options are available.	
Water overflows hazard posts – beyond posts is casual water	- free drop, 1 club length from nearest point of relief, not nearer the hole
Wrong Ball Played – a ball substituted.... (Whether intentionally or not) – Count stroke – play as lies – penalty 2 strokes – not your ball.... Don't count stroke – re-play – penalty 2 strokes – failure to re-play – disqualification	
Note: playing a ball moving in water, that is in fact a wrong ball, incurs no cost	

FURTHER ANSWERS ON PAGE 30

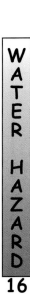

WATER HAZARD

INSTANT ANSWERS

THE GREEN (A ball is on the green when any part is on)

A ball is holed when it is at rest in the hole and fully below the top thereof.

Situation	Detail	Answer
Animal Holes/Scratchings - made by burrowing animals reptiles & birds	- ball in, or stroke or normal stance, or line of putt interfered by	- free place - nearest point of relief not nearer the hole & not in a hazard
Ball Interfering With or Assisting Any Player	- such ball(s) must be marked, if requested - failure to do so when requested	- penalty 2 strokes
Ball Marker Accidentally Moved	- marking or replacing ball, measuring, moving a loose impediment - other	- no penalty - replace marker - penalty 1 stroke
Ball Moves (also see p30)	- while marking or replacing ball, or removing marker, or measuring, removing loose impediments or movable obstructions, or repairing old holes or ball pitch marks	- no penalty - replace ball
	- before ball addressed - grounded club in front or back of ball - after ball addressed - not caused by player - other	- no penalty - play as lies - no penalty - play as lies - penalty -1 stroke - replace ball
Ball Overhangs Hole	- drops more than 10 seconds after player reaches hole (without undue delay)	- add 1 stroke
Ball Played From Off Green	- strikes another ball (from same group) - deflected by outside agency* (not deliberately) - deflected by outside agency* (deliberately)	- no penalty - play where lies - no penalty - play where lies - place where estimated would have stopped
	- picked-up by outside agency* * animal, human or equipment (not the players)	- place where picked-up (substitute ball if necessary - no penalty)
Ball Played From On Green	- strikes another ball (from same group)	- penalty 2 strokes if the ball is stopped or deflected by the other ball.
	- deflected by outside agency* - picked-up by outside agency*	- replay - replay - (substitute ball if necessary)
Ball Strikes Flag Stick - if resting on flag - remove flag - if ball drops it is holed	- played from off green - flag unattended - if attended	- no penalty - penalty 2 strokes - penalty 2 strokes
	- played from on green	
Casual Water	- free placing - nearest point of relief (which is not nearer the hole or in a hazard). If nearest relief is off the green then that is where the ball is placed.	
Cleaning Ball	- by rubbing on green	- penalty only if done to test green

Dropping		- ball is only dropped on green under "unplayable ball" and "lateral water hazard" penalty relief options. In all other situations it must be placed.
Growing Things	- removing without local rule	- penalty - 2 strokes
Immovable Obstructions (p40)	- relief - at nearest point of relief (not nearer the hole or in a hazard) - free place	
Line Of Putt	- touching in moving loose impediments or removable obstructions or in repairing pitch marks or old holes	- no penalty
	- standing on - accidentally, inadvertently, or to avoid standing on another players line of putt	- no penalty
	- touching or standing on other than above	- penalty - 2 strokes
Loose Impediments (p36) and Movable Obstructions (p38)	- remove before stroke	- no penalty
	- remove while ball in motion to avoid contact	- penalty - 2 strokes - exceptions - attended flag, flag on ground, & players' equipment.
Marking and Replacing Ball	- marking - allowed by anyone authorised by the player	
	- replacement - must be by the player or person who marked ball	
	- by anyone else - if not corrected	- penalty - 1 stroke
Order of Play	- furthest from hole.	- etiquette matter
	A player nearer the hole if requested to mark can putt instead	
Pitch Marks / Old Holes	- repair	- no penalty
Playing while a putt is in motion	- when not your turn	- penalty 2 strokes
Playing Moving Ball	- if ball commenced to move after back swing started there is no penalty.	- penalty - 2 strokes excepting that:
	- if you caused the ball to move see page 30 for possible "ball moved" penalty.	
Spike Marks	- to flatten spike marks in a players line of play	- penalty - 2 strokes
Testing Surface	- intentional testing by rolling a ball or rubbing the green	- penalty - 2 strokes
Wrong Ball Played	- a ball substituted.... (Whether intentionally or not) - Count stroke - play as lies - penalty 2 strokes	
	Don't count stroke - re-play - penalty 2 strokes	
	- not your ball.... - failure to re-play - disqualification	

FURTHER ANSWERS ON PAGE 30

THE GREEN

GOLFS PENALTIES
(Single Stroke & Stableford)

TWO STROKES

The penalty for infringements, where not otherwise stated in the rules, is "2 strokes." The incidences where other penalties apply include:

ONE STROKE

(1) Ball moved or caused to be moved by player
(2) Ball strikes the player or his/her equipment
(3) Casual water or immovable obstruction in bunker - dropping outside of bunker
(4) Cleaning ball when not permitted
(5) Double (or multiple) hit
(6) Dropping ball - in incorrect manner (if not corrected)
(7) Lifting ball without marking, or not giving marker or fellow competitor the opportunity to observe, or lifting when not necessary
(8) Marked ball replaced by wrong person   - if not corrected
(9) Using a tee other than from teeing area
(10) Putt drops after 10 seconds of overhanging hole
(11) Replacing a moved ball when not entitled
(12) Unplayable ball relief option
(13) Water hazard relief option

STROKE AND DISTANCE - 1 stroke penalty and re-play

(1) Ball out of bounds
(2) Lost ball

DISQUALIFICATION - in Stableford this generally means for the hole only

(1) Agreeing to waive rules
(2) Agreeing to play out of turn to secure an advantage
(3) Ball played from wrong place - if significant advantage obtained and not corrected
(4) Deliberately influencing position or movement of the ball or deliberately deflecting or stopping a ball
(5) Failing to hole out
(6) Having more than 1 caddie at any one time
(7) If Committee so decides... For:
  (a) agreeing with other competitors to not mark a ball that could assist another player if not marked.
  (b) a serious breach of etiquette
  (c) exerting influence on a ball where a significant advantage/disadvantage has resulted
(8) Playing holes outside correct order
(9) Practising on course on day of play prior to round - other than as permitted
(10) Refusing to comply with a rule affecting another players rights
(11) The tee - failing to arrive within 5 minutes of time appointed
       - deliberately moving tee markers
       - playing from outside teeing area (if not corrected)
(12) Score card   - failing to record handicap
       - recording higher than actual handicap
       - failing to record score
       - recording a lower than actual score for any hole
       - failing to sign card
       - failing to have marker sign card
(13) Second ball - having played but not reported to committee
(14) Unduly delaying or discontinuing play
(15) Using artificial devices, non-conforming balls or equipment, or clubs with deliberately changed characteristics
(16) Wrong ball played - failing to re-play with correct ball

23

NEAREST POINT OF RELIEF

In "2 club length" relief situations "nearest point of relief" is not a consideration, as measurement commences from the problem point, without reference to any nearest point of relief, and can be done with the club of choice; normally the driver.

For "one club length" relief situations, measurement does not commence at the problem point, but at the "nearest point of relief" from the problem point. How should this position be determined?

(1) Take the stance, direction of play and the club that would have been used, if the problem area had not existed.

(2) Swing the club, and determine the nearest point, from where a ball could be struck without interference to swing or *stance **by the problem area**. That point must not be nearer the hole nor on a putting green or in a hazard... except when taking relief in a hazard.

(3) The point where the ball would lie in that swing, is the "nearest point of relief", and the one club length measurement can be measured from that point with any club; usually the driver. It should be noted that we are not seeking the nearest point where an unrestricted stroke can be made.....only the point where the problem area does not interfere. That point may be in the middle of a bush or tree from which the 1 club length may still leave the player with little or no swing.

When taking relief from a staked tree the nearest point of relief will often bring the ball into proximity of another staked tree. The procedure cannot be abbreviated into finding nearest point of relief from the forest but must be done tree by tree. In some instances the nearest point of relief will be on an immovable obstruction such as a path. The ball must be dropped on the obstruction from which immovable obstruction relief can be then taken.

* When taking relief from a "wrong green", stance is not relevant, only swing.

Finding Nearest Point Of Relief

In this example the ball lies nearer to the right side of the path however the nearest point of relief is clearly on the left side i.e. the ball needs to be moved less to point "A" than to point "B".

Relief options..... for 1 stroke penalty, when a ball is in, or lost in, a:

YELLOW defined hazard - "water hazard"

(1) drop a ball behind the hazard (no limit on distance), at a point in line with where the ball last entered the hazard, and the flag.
(2) go back, and play from where the previous shot was played.

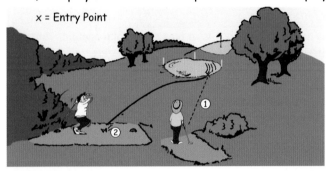

x = Entry Point

RED defined hazard - "lateral water hazard"

Options (1) and (2) above as for yellow defined, and 2 additional options: drop within 2 club lengths of:

(3) the point where the ball last entered the hazard, not nearer the hole.
(4) a point on the opposite side of the hazard, opposite to the point where the hazard was last crossed, equi-distant from the hole.

If it is not possible to drop within 2 club lengths, without being nearer the hole, these options are lost.

x = Entry Point

25

2012 SIGNIFICANT RULES AMENDMENTS

ADDRESSING THE BALL

Previously this was the taking of one's stance when in a hazard, and for elsewhere....., also grounding the club.

Now stance is not relevant...., and only the grounding of one's club, either in front of, or at the back of the ball, constitutes "addressing the ball". Accordingly, a ball in a hazard, now, never becomes "addressed".

All who firstly place their putter in front of the ball, will now be in the addressed position from that point.

BALL MOVES AFTER ADDRESSING – Previously an automatic penalty....

now no penalty when it is at least "virtually certain" that movement was not caused by the player.

ARRIVING LATE - Previously, after start time meant disqualification.

Now within 5 minutes, is a 2 stroke penalty, and 5 minutes onwards...... disqualification.

AMATEUR STATUS..... No longer lost through prizes won in hole in one

competitions, during a round of golf.

BALL LOST IN SAND - Previously raking or probing in sand, that resulted

in the ball moving, incurred no penalty if the ball was in a hazard. This relief has been extended to all parts of the course.

BALL IN HAZARD COVERED BY LOOSE, IMPEDIMENTS...., could

previously be searched for, with impunity. Not now, for if ball moves..... penalty 1 stroke.

BALL IN MOTION "DELIBERATELY" DEFLECTED OR STOPPED BY AN OUTSIDE AGENCY.

If the stroke was played from on the green, the stroke is replayed without penalty, as was previously the case.

If played from elsewhere, the place where it is estimated the ball would have come to rest, must be determined, and the ball dropped, if that position is through the green or in a hazard (or placed, if on the green).

If out of bounds, a normal out of bounds option must be selected.

SMOOTHING SAND OR SOIL IN A HAZARD. Previously only permitted

after stroke played. Now permitted before, provided not done to gain an advantage.

THE GOLF STROKE

What is a valid stroke?

A forward movement of the club at the players own ball made with the intention of hitting and moving the ball; but not including any swing voluntarily aborted. **The backswing is not part of a valid stroke.** Any infringements incurred in the backswing such as moving loose impediments in hazards, result in a penalty - 2 strokes. Strokes made other than "as defined" are not counted. An unintentional hit such as during a practice swing (at a ball in play) is not a valid stroke, nor is a swipe in anger. In both cases the stroke is not counted, but a 1 stroke penalty is incurred and the ball is replaced.

The manner of striking the ball is also regulated. The ball must not be pushed or scooped and must be struck at with the head of the club (either front, back or side). The penalty for infringing the striking regulations is 2 strokes.

BALL PLAYED FROM WRONG SPOT

THE GREEN

ASSISTANCE

OUT OF BOUNDS

A ball is out of bounds when all of the ball is beyond the course side of an out of bounds fence or otherwise designated boundary (at ground level).

When a ball is hit Out Of Bounds, the shot must be replayed by dropping a ball as near as possible to where the previous shot was played - penalty 1 stroke

The Out Of Bounds fence or posts are in fact Out Of Bounds, and no free relief is available from them.

Any ladder etc. on the course side of the fence is an immovable obstruction and relief is available - see page 40.

A ball that is not Out Of Bounds may be played from a stance Out Of Bounds.

FURTHER ANSWERS ON PAGE 30

ANYWHERE

Situation	Ruling
Advice - asking for or giving advice other than common knowledge and distance	- penalty 2 strokes
Assistance - accepting assistance while playing a shot such as protection from weather, indicating line of putt etc.	- penalty 2 strokes
Ball deflected by outside agency (animal, human or equipment - other than the players) - if deliberately deflected, drop where estimated ball would have stopped	- played from off the green - otherwise play as lies
Ball Moved but returns to original spot	- no penalty excepting *
Ball Moved but doesn't return	
- moved by another ball or an outside agency (animal, human or equipment - other than the players) - replace ball	
- moved or caused to be moved by the player (or players equipment)	
- accidentally in:	
- marking or replacing ball, or measuring	- no penalty - replace ball
- searching in g.u.r. or other abnormal ground such as casual water, or in or on an obstruction (but not when in water hazard).	- no penalty - replace ball
- practice swing (when ball is "in play")	- penalty 1 stroke - replace ball
- removing loose impediments (when not on green)	- penalty 1 stroke - replace ball
- removing movable obstructions	- no penalty - replace ball
* - picking up or touching other than where permitted by the rules *	- penalty 1 stroke
- other than above	- penalty 1 stroke - replace ball
Ball Played From Wrong Spot	
- no significant advantage obtained - play as lies	- penalty 2 strokes inclusive of any associated "ball moved" penalty
- significant advantage obtained - if not replayed	- disqualification
Ball Rolls - before ball addressed (not caused by the player)	- no penalty - play as lies
- after ball addressed - (unless virtually certain not caused by player)	- penalty 1 stroke - replace ball
Ball Strikes Other Players Person or Equipment (Played from off green)	- no penalty - play as lies
Ball Strikes the Player or Player's Equipment	- penalty 1 stroke - play as lies
Ball taken by outside agency (animal or human)	
- Ball in motion - played from off green	- replace where estimated would have stopped
- played from on green	- replay
- Ball stationary	- replace where taken
Ball Unfit for Play - ball may be marked, lifted, examined (not cleaned) replaced - (if unfit for use)	- with markers consent - no penalty - without markers consent - penalty 1 stroke
Clubs - borrowing from other players or carrying more than 14 or any non-conforming clubs	- penalty 2 strokes per hole (max 4 str.)
- using club damaged through normal use	- no penalty
- using club damaged through misuse	- disqualification
- applying tape/gauze to assist gripping the club	- disqualification
- using towel or handkerchief to help grip	- no penalty

Topic	Description	Ruling
Discontinuing Play (without committee authorisation)	- bad weather - lightning/emergencies	- disqualification - committee may approve
Double or Multiple Hits	- count stroke and	- penalty 1 stroke
Equity	- if no rule covers a situation then what would be fair under the circumstances should apply. eg. to avoid wildlife	- free drop
Exerting Influence on Ball Including:	- picking up loose impediments, movable obstructions or a ball in play to avoid a ball in motion	- penalty 2 strokes - exceptions - attended flag, flag on ground, and players' equipment. (A ball in play or its marker/coin is not "equipment".)
Improving Lie, Stance, Area of Intended Swing, Dropping Area, or Line of Play	- in fairly taking stance - in making stroke (forward movement) - in backswing of a completed stroke - otherwise, including: - removing sand, soil, immovable obstructions, casual water, dew, frost - bending or breaking grass, flowers, twigs, branches - leveling or pressing down sand soil divot's spike marks or building a stance - shaking water from bushes, trees	- no penalty - no penalty - no penalty expect when in hazard 2 stroke - penalty 2 strokes, excepting, that on the green, sand and soil can be removed and pitch marks and old holes repaired, and on the tee making or removing ground irregularities is permitted.
Line of Sight - immovable obstruction inhibiting vision		- no relief (unless by local rule)
Lost Ball - in G.U.R. or an obstruction (must be virtually certain)	- other - search time - 5 minutes from player/caddy commencing search. The ball remains the ball in play until 5 minutes elapses or the ball is replaced; i.e. a stroke is made at a substituted ball. Time playing a wrong ball is excluded. - a ball located after 5 minutes becomes a wrong ball if played - failure to rectify	- free relief, see p10, p38 or p40 - penalty 1 stroke and replay from where previous stroke played. If lost in a water hazard other options available (p16) - penalty 2 strokes - disqualification
Marking Ball	- if requested by a player, ball must be marked even in hazards (If lie is interfered with by a players stroke, it may be restored)	- failure to so do - penalty 2 strokes
Order of Play	- furthest from hole - regardless of whether on green or not	- etiquette matter
Practice Chipping & Putting (during course round - not holding up play)	- on green completed, teeing area of next hole, or practice area - other than above	- no penalty (unless by local rule) - penalty 2 strokes
Waiving Rules	- agreeing to do so including failure to apply known penalty	- disqualification
Wrong Green	- ball must be dropped off green - 1 club length (p42)	- penalty 2 strokes if played from green

My ball has rolled near that kangaroo. If I go over there it might attack me.

Where no rule exists for a dangerous situation the rule of equity applies. You may either pick up the ball or select another ball and drop at the nearest safe spot. However as your ball is in a hazard you must drop in a hazard else you will incur a 1 stroke penalty.

IMPROVING SWING AREA

I've knocked some leaves down with my practice swing. Is that a penalty Doug?

Not necessarily Russell. You are only penalised if the removal of those leaves has improved your swing area. I don't believe your swing area has been improved.

BALL HITS EQUIPMENT

Oh! My shot has hit your bag and ricocheted onto mine.

That's tough Russell. There's no penalty for hitting mine, but a 1 stroke penalty for hitting your own.

INSTANT ANSWERS   -   FAIRWAY & ROUGH - PAGES 4 & 30

BAD WEATHER

LINE OF SIGHT

ADVICE

LOOSE IMPEDIMENTS

LOOSE IMPEDIMENTS

Loose impediments are natural objects that are not fixed and not growing.
They include: - dung
- grass clippings (not piled for removal), leaves & branches
- dead birds & animals
- rocks and stones
- worms and insects (and their mounds)

Loose impediments can be removed without penalty (excepting from hazards)

Loose impediments must be "loose" not solidly embedded and not adhering to the ball. Rocks can be loose impediments and help to remove them is permitted if done without undue delay. Leaves etc. stuck to a ball can only be removed on the green or when cleaning the ball in relief situations.

Sand and soil are loose impediments only on the putting green.

Snow and natural ice are both loose impediments and casual water at the players option.

Frost and dew are not loose impediments and they provide no relief.

If, through the green, a ball rolls as a result of removing a loose impediment a 1 stroke penalty results and the ball must be replaced. On the green - no penalty.

MOVABLE OBSTRUCTIONS

Movable obstructions are similar to loose impediments in that they are easily movable, the principal difference being that loose impediments are natural and movable obstructions artificial.
Movable obstructions include:
- bottles and cans
- hoses
- ice (manufactured)
- planks
* - stakes - easily moved (internal only, not out of bounds)
- tools
* Unless declared immovable by local rule

Movable obstructions can be removed without penalty anywhere on the course.

Movable obstructions provide 2 advantages over loose impediments. They can be removed from hazards - loose impediments cannot, and secondly, if a ball moves as a result of removing an obstruction no penalty is incurred. With loose impediments immunity is granted only on the green.

A ball resting on or in a movable obstruction should be lifted, the obstruction removed, and the ball dropped (or on a green placed) as near as possible to its original position.

When a ball is lost in a movable obstruction no penalty results, and a ball is dropped, (or on the green placed) at the nearest possible point below where the obstruction was last entered, not nearer the hole.

Loose Impediments	Movable Obstructions	Immovable Obstructions
Don't remove in hazards	Remove anywhere	Don't remove anywhere
Stones	Bottles	Shed
Leaves	Cans	Internal fence
Sticks, branches, pine cones	Rakes	Roads & paths with artificial surfaces
Insects	Car (if unlocked)	Car (if locked)
Dead animals	Hoses	Taps

MOVABLE OBSTRUCTIONS

38

IMMOVABLE OBSTRUCTIONS

These are artificial obstructions not easily moved, such as:
- internal fencing, sheds
- roads and paths (containing artificial materials)
- sprinkler heads, taps (faucets)
- stakes not easily moved (internal only - not O.O.B.)

Ball in, on, or swing or normal stance interfered by.
Relief - Where a ball is in:
(1) A water hazard - no free relief available.
(2) Any other part of the course - free relief - excepting, that:
   (i) Where it is clearly unreasonable to play a stroke because of some other factor such as a tree or roots, or
   (ii) The obstruction only interferes as a result of taking an abnormal stance, swing or direction of play, then . . . free relief is not available (see page 44).
The "where is your ball" pages record the manner in which relief is to be taken.

On the green, relief is also available from an obstruction on the line of putt.

Stakes (other than o.o.b. stakes) can be movable or immovable depending on how easily removable. Many clubs declare stakes to be immovable by local rule.

Paths and tracks of natural materials (dirt/clay) are not obstructions and no relief is available.

When taking relief, stance must be clear of the obstruction.

When a ball is lost in an immovable obstruction (other than in a water hazard) no penalty results and normal relief applies - relief is from estimated last entry point.

No relief is available for "line of sight". One club length from nearest point of physical relief is all that is available. Line of sight is only available where provided by local rule.

DROPPING BALL (relief situations)

How to Drop. In all cases, the ball must be dropped (not spun) from an erect stance and with an extended arm at shoulder height. It must strike the ground within the allowable area but may travel for up to a further 2 club lengths (not nearer the hole than the problem point or nearest point of relief) without requiring re-dropping. The ball can therefore finish as much as four club lengths from the problem point.

Where to Drop. The circumstances where relief dropping apply are shown on the "Where is Your Ball?" pages. Turn to the page for the part of the course where your ball lies.

Finding Nearest Point of Relief - Applicable to only 1 club length drops (see page 24)

Measuring Relief Dropping Area - One and two club length drops can be measured with the club of choice. One club length measures are from the "nearest point of relief"; two club lengths measures from the problem point itself.

When to Re-Drop. Re-dropping is required if the dropped ball:
  (1) comes to rest more than 2 club lengths from where dropped
  (2) comes to rest nearer the hole than the point of relief or problem point
  (3) rolls back inside the area from which relief is being taken
       (other than in the case of "unplayable ball" drops where this misfortune must be accepted)
  (4) rolls onto a green or into or out of a hazard
  (5) rolls out of bounds
  (6) strikes a player or players' equipment
  (7) was incorrectly dropped or dropped in a wrong place
If after re-dropping, proper relief has not resulted, (i.e. any of (1) to (5) above apply) the ball must be placed where the second drop landed. This is not the case where (6) or (7) applies, in which case, the ball is again re-dropped.
When dropping in a declared "dropping zone" the ball may roll outside the designated area; up to 2 club lengths from where striking the ground.

G.U.R and Immovable Obstructions. When dropping from G.U.R. or an immovable obstruction, a legal drop must result in the players stance being fully outside the G.U.R. or obstruction. No such requirement exists for dropping from **Hazards**; in which case re-dropping to ensure stance is clear of the hazard would incur a 2 stroke penalty and possible disqualification (see page 30 - ball played from wrong spot).

Markers (Scorer) Observance. A ball must never be lifted without firstly offering one's marker or fellow competitor to observe. Penalty for failure to do so – 1 stroke. If the marker does not believe that free relief is available, then the original ball should be played as lies and a second ball (nominated as the preferred ball) dropped and also played, for later decision by the committee.

43

UNPLAYABLE BALL

A ball can be declared unplayable anywhere on the course excepting when in a water hazard - penalty one stroke.

To do so provides the following options:

Through the green (fairway & rough)

(1) drop within two club lengths of where ball rests (not nearer the hole). For relief from large trees or bush areas this may not provide adequate relief.

(2) drop behind where the ball rests (no limit on distance) keeping that point between the drop point and the flag.

(3) play from place of previous shot.

If option (1) is taken but the drop does not result in full relief, a free re-drop is not permitted. This is the case even should the ball return to its original unplayable position.

Bunkers

Same as above excepting under options (1) and (2), the ball must be dropped in the bunker.

> My ball is unplayable. Can I bring it out past the branches if I declare it unplayable?

> No Russell - you can only move it sideways up to 2 club lengths of where it lies. There are of course other options available to you under the unplayable ball options.

> I'm stymied behind this tree but fortunately I'm entitled to relief from the rabbit holes so I'll take a free drop.

> No you won't Russell. There are exceptions to the rule that gives relief from abnormal ground and obstructions; which preclude free relief if it is clearly unreasonable to play a stroke because of any other condition. There is no doubt this big tree and roots is exactly what this exception is about. In addition you would have to take an exaggerated stance to be in those holes and such action again precludes a free drop.

Exception to relief from abnormal ground and obstructions

UNPLAYABLE BALL

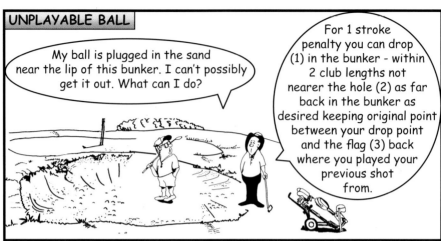

My ball is plugged in the sand near the lip of this bunker. I can't possibly get it out. What can I do?

For 1 stroke penalty you can drop (1) in the bunker - within 2 club lengths not nearer the hole (2) as far back in the bunker as desired keeping original point between your drop point and the flag (3) back where you played your previous shot from.

LOST BALL FOUND

Don't hit that ball Doug. I've found your original ball and five minutes haven't elapsed.

Thank you Russell. This ball has not become my ball in play. Making a stroke at a substituted ball is what makes it the ball in play.

PROVISIONAL BALL

I'll look for you Russell and if I find it within 5 minutes it will be your ball in play whether you like it or not. You should not have called the second ball a provisional ball if you didn't want to find the first.

I've hit a provisional ball from the tee because I'm sure my original ball will be lost in that wooded area. I'm not even going to look for the original ball as I know it will be impossible to play.

PROVISIONAL BALL

When to play: A provisional ball may be played, if it is considered that the ball played *may* be out of bounds or *may* be lost outside of a water hazard.

When not to play: A provisional ball cannot be played if:
  (1) The ball played is definitely in a water hazard, or
  (2) The player has gone forward to search for the ball.
It is not possible to "go back" to play a provisional ball. Any ball played in such circumstances becomes the ball in play regardless of the status of the previous ball. The point at which the original ball becomes "out of play" is when a stroke is made at another ball or the five minute search time has elapsed.

If a provisional ball is played, and it is subsequently determined that the original ball *was* lost in a water hazard, there are no repercussions. The original ball is in play under the water hazard rules and the provisional ball is picked up without cost.

Where a provisional ball has been played, it may be hit as a provisional ball until the anticipated position of the original ball is reached. If the original ball is then found, it is the ball in play, whether desired or not, and the provisional ball ceases to exist (with no cost). If it is not found, the provisional ball is the ball in play. The penalty for the loss of the original ball, the stroke that caused it to be lost, and the stroke with the provisional ball result in the player recording 3 strokes, for a distance hoped for in 1 stroke.

When first playing a provisional ball, it is essential to advise ones marker that a provisional ball is to be played. Failure to do so results in the ball becoming the ball in play and the original ball being treated as lost.

ETIQUETTE

What does it mean?

Do unto others as you would have them do unto you.

Don't disturb or distract other players or in any way interfere with their right to play without harassment or intimidation.

Be safety concious at all times; careful to never endanger others.

Be disciplined, courteous and sportsmanlike; not given to club throwing or other bad mannered or aggressive behaviour.

Be considerate of those following by allowing others to play through if your group is unable to keep up with those ahead.

Take care of the course, minimising damage wherever possible.
Repair divot holes you have made, pitch marks on greens and on completion of any hole any damage caused by golf shoes. Bunkers should be smoothed or raked after exiting. Care should be taken not to damage putting greens or putting green holes. Balls should not be removed fom holes with club heads.

Penalty for breach of acceptable etiquette standards.

The committee may:

- for consistent disregard during a round or over a period of time, take disciplinary action including prohibiting an offender from course or competition play for a penalty period.
- for a serious breach, disqualify an offender.

Don't stand where your presence may upset a player that is making a stroke.